Copyright © 1993 Irwin Publishing

Canadian Cataloguing in Publication Data
Main entry under title:

Convincing ideas

(Irwin Writing Project)
ISBN 0-7725-1923-4

1. Creative writing – Juvenile literature.
2. English language – Composition and exercises –
Juvenile literature. I. Rich, Sharon. II. Series.

LB1576.C66 1993   808'.0427   C92-095420-0

DESIGN: Matthews Communications Design
PROJECT EDITOR: Maryjean Lancefield
ILLUSTRATORS: William Kimber, Stuart Knox, Lilian
Lampert, Sharon Matthews, Elfriede Parkyn
PHOTOGRAPHER: Vivian Gast

ACKNOWLEDGEMENTS
2: Courtesy of Jim Benton (Dream of a Pure Planet)
Beatrice Foods Inc., Canada 125 Corp., Friends of
the Earth, General Publishing Ltd., Heinemann
International   **4:** We wish to thank the Metropolitan
Toronto Works Department for permission to use
their material. **16:** Courtesy of W.K. Buckley Limited
17: Courtesy of Beatrice Foods Inc. **23:** Used by
permission of General Publishing Ltd.

Printed in Canada on Provincial Papers' Eco Matte
Recycled Stock and bound by the Bryant Press.

CONVINCING

Ideas

Sharon J. Rich
Elaine M. Crocker
Helen G. Langford
Kathleen Rosborough

CONSULTANT
Terry MacKenzie

D1416537

Irwin Publishing
Toronto, Canada

LOOK

at the collage.

WHAT

do all of the items in the collage have in common? These slogans, advertisements, letters, and book descriptions are all trying to persuade someone to do something.

LIST

the ones you think are most effective in your Writer's Notebook.

SLOGANS

Slogans are used for different purposes.
These slogans are trying to persuade us to care
about our planet. Think about something you
could do to help protect your environment.
It might be to pick up litter on the playground.
It could be to recycle waste from the lunchroom.

What else could it be?

BEYOND THE BLUE BOX

HOW TO GET RID OF OBNOXIOUS HOUSE GUESTS

Be Good to Your Garden

CHECK IT OUT BEFORE YOU CHUCK IT OUT.

Creating Your Own
SLOGAN

In a small group, talk about something that is important to you. It could be an idea to help protect the environment or something else.

Now that you have discussed some ideas with your group, you might want to take these ideas and work on your own or with a partner. You could think of a slogan you could use to convince others that your idea is a good one. You might have one slogan or you might have several.

In your Writer's Notebook, jot down your favourite slogan. Ask a friend about the message in your slogan. Does the slogan get your idea across clearly? Does your friend know what the message of the slogan is?

Decide how you will share your slogan with others. You might design a button or a poster or a bumper sticker or.... Share your draft design with a friend. Ask your friend about the lettering and the spacing. Once you are satisfied with your draft, you may wish to complete a final copy to display in your classroom.

To make your own pin

- Choose a medium-size lid from a jar.

- Use the lid to trace a circle onto stiff cardboard. Cut out the circle.

- Puncture small holes and push a safety pin through the cardboard circle.

- Tape the pin in place on the circle.

- Insert the cardboard circle and safety pin into the underside of the lid.

- Glue your picture, paper collage, or Plasticine art onto the front of the lid.

WRITERS' TIPS

- Keep your words simple and direct. ("Recycle Now" is easier to remember than "We Want You To Recycle Now.")

- Print clearly.

- Leave enough space between words so the reader can read your message quickly.

- Check your message with a friend.

- Ask your friend about the lettering and spacing.

- Make your message clear and readable!

— cleaning up our world starts with you
— poster

IF WE ALL WORK TOGETHER WE CAN MAKE A DIFFERENCE

— pin

clean it up!

clean it up!

CONVINCING Letters

Writing letters is another way of trying to convince others to do something. In a letter you can tell your reader why you want him or her to act in a particular way.

The following letters were written by some children. Read each letter and, with a partner, discuss what each writer wants.

Dear Editor,

   We talked about the blue box in our class. We think it is important to use the blue boxes for glass and paper.

   In our class, we counted bits of garbage we throw away at lunchtime. There are twenty-five children in our class. We had 240 bits of garbage wraps from lunch. That's a lot of garbage! We decided to have a garbage-free lunch day. Each of us brought our lunch in containers we could use again. We had only twenty bits of garbage.

   We want everyone to know that they can help the garbage problem. You just have to get a good idea.

                    Sincerely,

                    Amanda Finch

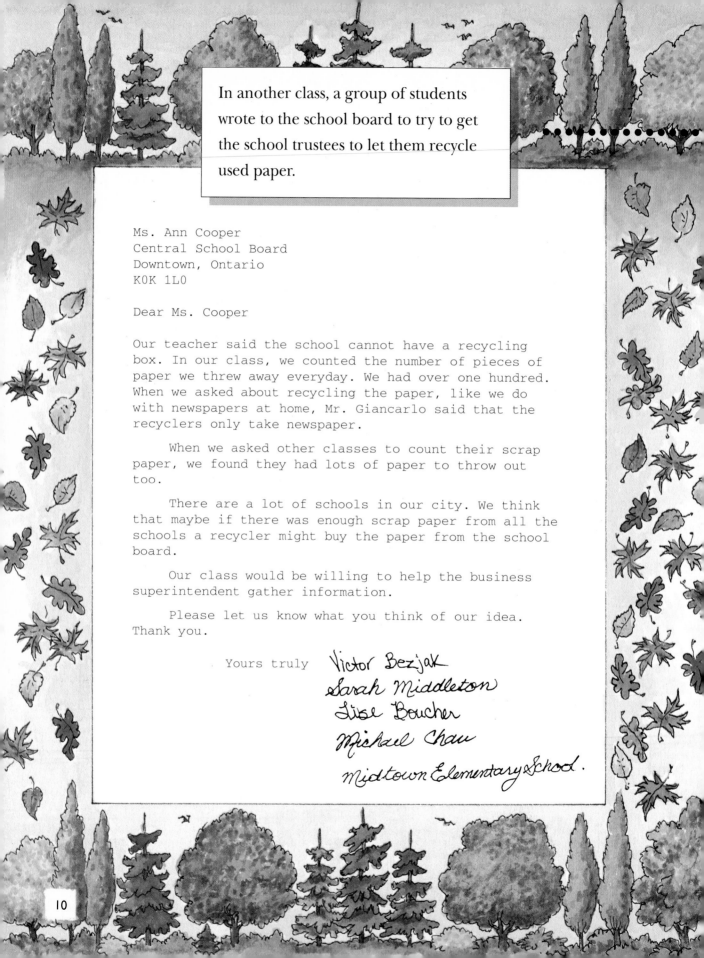

In another class, a group of students wrote to the school board to try to get the school trustees to let them recycle used paper.

Ms. Ann Cooper
Central School Board
Downtown, Ontario
K0K 1L0

Dear Ms. Cooper

Our teacher said the school cannot have a recycling box. In our class, we counted the number of pieces of paper we threw away everyday. We had over one hundred. When we asked about recycling the paper, like we do with newspapers at home, Mr. Giancarlo said that the recyclers only take newspaper.

When we asked other classes to count their scrap paper, we found they had lots of paper to throw out too.

There are a lot of schools in our city. We think that maybe if there was enough scrap paper from all the schools a recycler might buy the paper from the school board.

Our class would be willing to help the business superintendent gather information.

Please let us know what you think of our idea. Thank you.

Yours truly   Victor Bezjak
Sarah Middleton
Lise Boucher
Michael Chau
Midtown Elementary School.

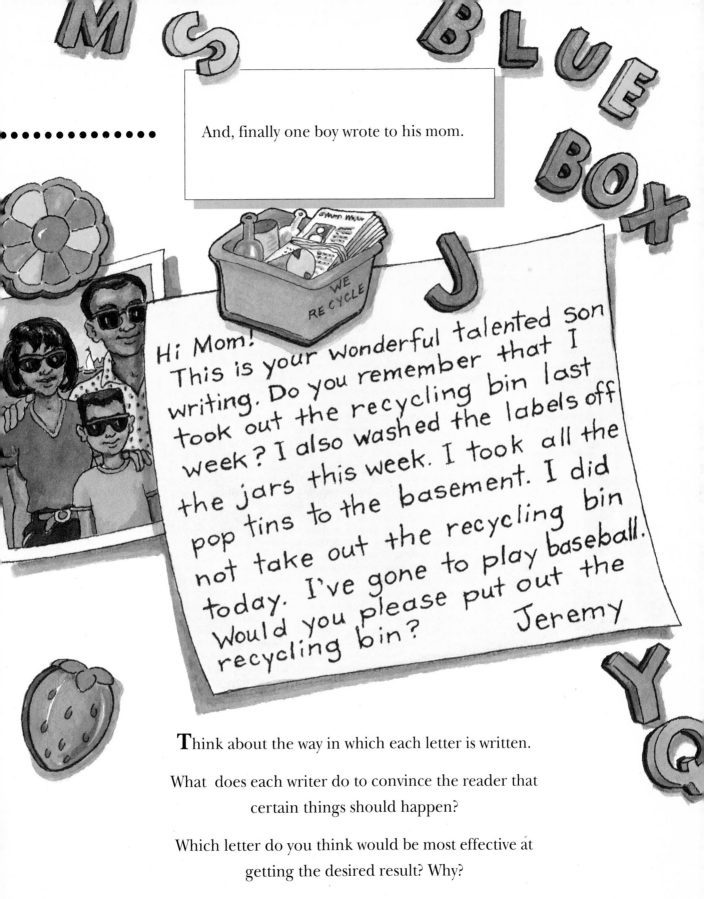

And, finally one boy wrote to his mom.

Hi Mom! This is your wonderful talented son writing. Do you remember that I took out the recycling bin last week? I also washed the labels off the jars this week. I took all the pop tins to the basement. I did not take out the recycling bin today. I've gone to play baseball. Would you please put out the recycling bin?

Jeremy

Think about the way in which each letter is written.

What does each writer do to convince the reader that certain things should happen?

Which letter do you think would be most effective at getting the desired result? Why?

Writing a CONVINCING LETTER

Think about something you would like to persuade someone to do. The someone could be a parent, a guardian, a friend, a brother or sister, or even the prime minister!

Brainstorm your ideas with a partner. Discuss the reasons you would need to give to someone to make him or her do what you want.

In your Writer's Notebook, you might want to make a chart of what you want someone to do and why she or he should do it. Your chart might look like this one.

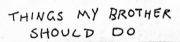

THINGS MY BROTHER SHOULD DO	WHY?
• lend me his binoculars	• because I want to do a project on birds

When you have thought about your reasons, write a letter or note to your selected audience. What do you think might happen if you have been very convincing?

13

...you could convince anyone in the world to do whatever you wanted. Who would you convince to do what?

Advertisements

Most people have seen ads similar to the ones on these two pages. Some of the ads are old; some are new. Some of the ads were drawn by students.

What do the ads try to get you to do?

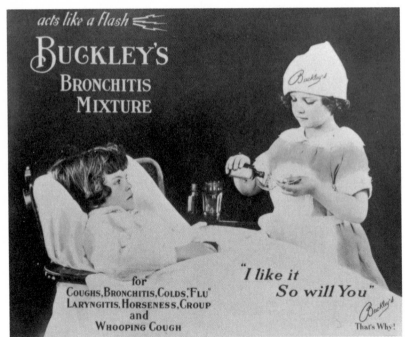

Start a class collection of your favourite or least favourite ads. Pick some of the slogans or songs used in the ads and improvise with new words or lyrics.

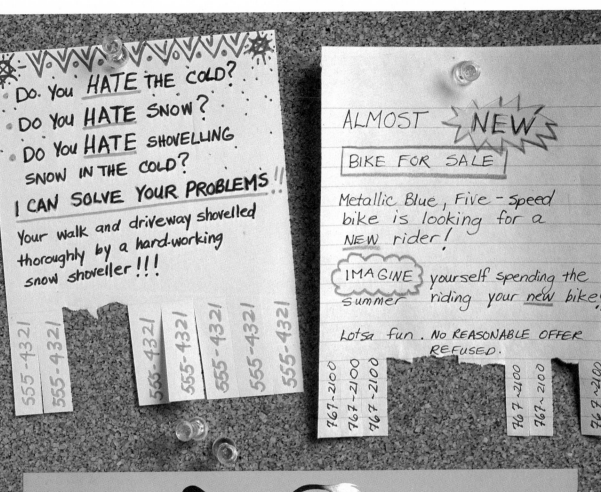

Do you HATE THE COLD?
Do you HATE SNOW?
Do you HATE SHOVELLING SNOW IN THE COLD?
I CAN SOLVE YOUR PROBLEMS!!

Your walk and driveway shovelled thoroughly by a hard-working snow shoveller!!!

555-4321
555-4321
555-4321
555-4321
555-4321
555-4321

ALMOST **NEW**

BIKE FOR SALE

Metallic Blue, Five-speed bike is looking for a NEW rider!

IMAGINE yourself spending the summer riding your new bike!!

Lotsa fun. NO REASONABLE OFFER REFUSED.

767-2100
767-2100
767-2100
767-2100
767-2100
767-2100

TRUE TO MOO

Beatrice

Creating an
ADVERTISEMENT

When advertisers want to sell a product, they think about what the product is. Then they decide who might want to buy the product. They also want to give a reason for someone to buy their product. They try to make people think that the product they have for sale is extra special.

With a partner, decide on a product that you could sell to your classmates, to your teacher, or to your family.

Brainstorm reasons why people might buy your product. Think about words that you might use to describe the product. Jot down your ideas in your Writer's Notebook.

Once you have some good ideas, begin to write an advertisement for your product. Decide whether your advertisement will be on radio, in the newspaper, in a magazine, or on television. Remember, you are only drafting your advertisement, so now is the time to think about what you want to say.

Exchange your advertisement
with your partner.
Ask yourself:

- Did this advertisement get my
  attention?

- Was the name of the product
  mentioned?

- Are the words effective?

- Did the advertisement make me want
  to buy the product?

Think about the suggestions your
partner gave you. Now revise your
advertisement.

Think about how an advertiser might make the following words more colourful:

red   fast   tasty

Choose one of the words to use in an advertisement. Make up one or two phrases using it. Can anyone guess what product you're describing?

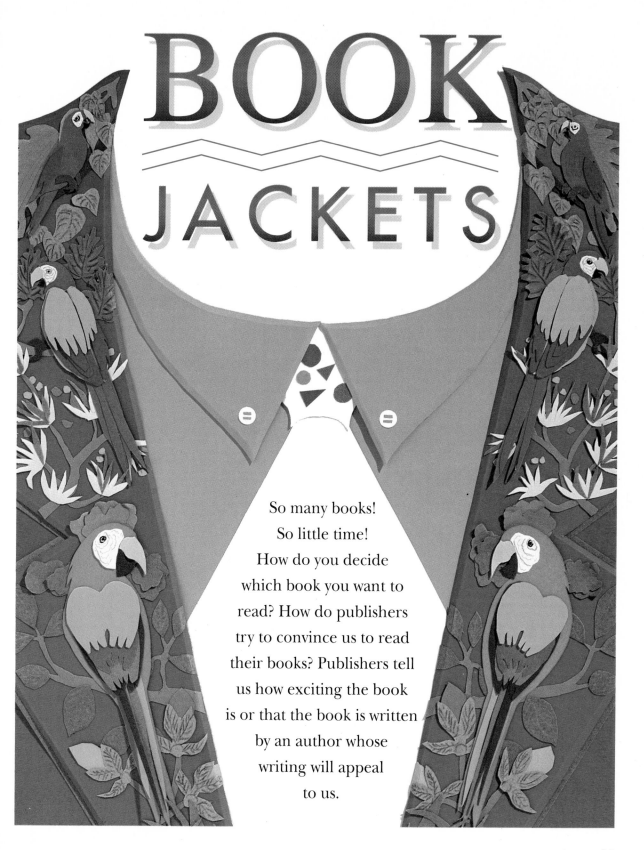

BOOK JACKETS

So many books!
So little time!
How do you decide
which book you want to
read? How do publishers
try to convince us to read
their books? Publishers tell
us how exciting the book
is or that the book is written
by an author whose
writing will appeal
to us.

Writing a
BOOK JACKET
DESCRIPTION

Look at your class library and read some
of the book jacket descriptions. Why did
you select one book over another? How
would you convince someone to read
your favourite book?

In your Writer's Notebook, list some of
your favourite books. Beside the title,
suggest some reasons why people might
want to read the book.

Think of a way to present your
description. You might want to draw a
jacket for your favourite book and write
your personal review of the book on the
back of the jacket. You could make
a class display of your
book jackets for
the school library.

IT'S UP TO US

T I M E T R A C K S # 1

(Originally published as *Fusion Factor*)

Twelve-year-old Rebecca lives in Winnipeg. Her biggest problem is a "D" her teacher gave her. And it all happened because her arch-enemy Lonney Dorman refused to cooperate.

Early one morning, Rebecca doesn't even like kidnapped. Although Rebecca doesn't even like Lonney, she won't rest until she finds the black van and the two goons who took him away.

Now she finds herself dealing with a time machine, chemical and nuclear war, and secret military bases . . .

Carol Matas lives in Winnipeg, where she was born and raised. When she was 20 she went to London, to study acting, and then worked as an actor in Toronto. In 1988 her novel, *Lisa*, won the Geoffrey Bilson Award for Historical Fiction.

The TimeTracks Series:

#1 *It's Up to Us*
#2 *Zanu*

THE HOUSE THAT MAX BUILT

"Think of it," Maxwell Holman III chanted, "sixty glorious days, two whole months, one sixth of an entire year with no homework, no teachers, and no more tuna sandwiches. It boggles the mind!"

Summer holidays start promisingly as Max and his friends Perky and Amanda build a magnificent house out of cardboard boxes.

And then things get even better. One of the rooms has magical qualities! Soon it transports them back to history in the making — the days of King Arthur and his knights — and the threesome discover who their friend John Marmalade really is . . .

JOHN GREEN is also the author of *There's a Dragon in Closet, Alice and the Birthday Giant*, and *Junkpile Jennifer*.

AMAZING WORLDS

AMAZING CATS

A fascinating look at some of the world's most amazing cats.

• Why do leopards have spots?
• Which cat likes swimming?
• How can you tell when a cat is angry?

These are just some of the surprises to be found in **Amazing Worlds**, a fresh approach to the marvels and mysteries of the world around us. Superb close-up photographs and colourful artwork show the world in amazing detail, as if through a magnifying glass.

Other titles in the series include:

Why not start a favourite book bulletin board? You and your classmates could post reviews of your favourite books. Other students who read the books could add their comments to your review. At the end of the month, conduct a class survey to find out which book is the favourite in your classroom.

REVISITING

You have had the chance to use writing to persuade other people to do things, to read something, or to buy something. Now go through your writing and select the piece that you think is the most convincing.

On a separate sheet of paper, write down why you have selected this piece of writing. Make a note of what you have done well in this piece. It might be that you have used very descriptive words. It might be that you have used a terrific idea. It might be that your drawing and writing go well together.

Now go back through your writing and find one piece that you could improve. What would you change in this piece? What would you keep the same?

Sometimes writers have ideas that don't always work well. Sometimes they put these ideas away and revisit them later. Make some notes about changes you would make in this piece of writing, then put it in the rough draft or work-in-progress section of your Writing Folder.

Did you read any writing by anyone in your class that really persuaded you to do something or to think in a new way?

What makes it difficult to convince someone to do something in writing?